# PETS AT THE WHITE HOUSE

By CARL CARMER

*Illustrated by Sam Savitt*

The unpretentious dog, horse, and parrot are among the wide variety of tame animals who kept the celebrated company of our country's leaders. In this delightfully illustrated book, Carl Carmer relates the fascinating stories of the favorite pets of ten Presidents and their families.

Here are behind-the-scene glimpses of Martha Washington riding her horse up and down the stairs of a sedate house . . . Tad Lincoln driving a herd of goats through the East Room of the executive mansion . . . Thomas Jefferson feeding his mocking-bird . . . Zack Taylor's horse, "Old Whitey," upsetting a dignified parade.

$2.95

# PETS AT THE WHITE HOUSE

FOR

*Herbert Henry Gibbs*

AND

*Carl Carmer Gibbs*

The tales are arranged chrono-logically, starting with President Washington and ending with President Eisenhower, and each is set against a background of the historical events of the period.

PETS AT THE WHITE HOUSE gives the honor due these loyal and devoted animals, and demonstrates how their companionship may have had an influence—however slight—on the great men who guided our country through history.

*Books by Carl Carmer*

HURRICANE LUCK

PETS AT THE WHITE HOUSE

# PETS AT THE
# WHITE HOUSE

### by Carl Carmer

ILLUSTRATED BY
**Sam Savitt**

E. P. DUTTON & CO., INC. ~ NEW YORK
1959

# CONTENTS

* This spelling was preferred by Mrs. Madison.

# FOREWORD

The old adage, "A cat may look at a king," has always assumed that the cat would get some pleasure from the experience. The reverse of the saying is equally true because in the world's history many a high-placed official —including Dick Whittington who became Lord Mayor of London—has acquired both enjoyment and inspiration from observing his cat.

The tame animals who have offered their loyalty and devotion to the American Presidents have not, I think, ever been given appropriate honor. The companionship of dog, parrot, horse, mockingbird has given those troubled men, who have been designated by the American public to lead the country, moments of recreation from which they have turned to their important problems with refreshed minds and clearer perspectives.

The purpose of this little book is to relate the histories of some of these lowly but important animals and to make evident how their companionship may have had an influence, however slight, on the progress of the United States during the years of its existence.

CARL CARMER

# PETS AT THE WHITE HOUSE

# 1: THE PETS OF THE WASHINGTONS

In this book the name White House is used to symbolize the dwelling of the President of the United States. George Washington, the first President, lived in a brick house at 10 Cherry Street, New York City, immediately after he was inaugurated and it was called "The President's Palace." When the seat of government was moved to Philadelphia, the Washingtons lived there at 190 High Street, a house bearing the same title. Even after the city of Washington was chosen as the nation's capital, and a house expressly for the residence of the President was built on the site where the White House now stands, it was still called a palace. Only after that house was burned by an invading British Army in 1815 and a new and snowy-pillared mansion replaced it, was the house of the President, then James Madison, known as "the White House."

When George Washington married Martha Dandridge Custis, however, the ceremony took place in a Maryland plantation dwelling which the bride had inherited from her dead husband, Daniel Parke Dandridge, and it is an interesting fact that it had long borne the name, "the White House." The happy couple lived there for several

months before George took Martha to his own Mount
Vernon.

Both Martha and George were fond of animal companions. General Braddock, before he died in the battle against
the French and Indians, gave his favorite horse to the
young colonial major whose good advice he had failed to
follow, and George cherished this mount as a memento
of his gallant though unwise commander. As for Martha,
she had been born and reared in New Kent County in rural
Virginia, and the fact that she was an expert horsewoman
had been attested by her gaily riding her horse Fatima up
one staircase and down another in Esling Green, the sedate
home of her admiring uncle, William Dandridge. Before
she married Daniel Custis, an admirer had tamed a mockingbird for her and her owning of the caged gray singer
was to set a precedent for at least two other wives of American Presidents.

After the Revolution and before General Washington
became President there were many pets at Mount Vernon
—among them Nelson, the great warrior's favorite battle
charger which he had ridden on the day of the surrender
of Cornwallis at Yorktown. He was variously described
as "pale brown" or "chestnut" and his markings included a
white face. A well-tamed animal, he would come to the
pasture fence at his master's call. There was a pack of
hounds, too, at Mount Vernon—sent by the Marquis de
Lafayette, who also sent a brace of colorful Chinese pheas-
ants to beautify the lawn. Vulcan, another dog, was too
much of an individual to be kept with the hounds, and

got himself into history by stealing a whole ham from the cookhouse and dodging his way into his kennel where he devoured it. Martha had also acquired a parrot, which made the circuit from Mount Vernon to New York to Philadelphia and return. The High Street "Palace" had a stable containing stalls for twelve horses and the President often rode with his little grandson.

For seven years the Washingtons lived in Philadelphia. Then on a March day after the inauguration of John Adams they set out for Mount Vernon in a crowded coach containing not only themselves but their two grandchildren and General Washington's namesake George Washington de Lafayette, and that young Frenchman's tutor. Behind them, even more overloaded, rattled the baggage wagon with all the trunks and other last-minute articles piled high. Above the heap the parrot screamed in dismay and a pet dog barked.

At a stop on their way home George Washington wrote a letter to his secretary Tobias Lear whom he had left behind in Philadelphia. Like many another husband and father he had become harried and cross on moving day.

"On one side," he wrote, "I am called upon to remember the parrot, and on the other, to remember the dog. For my own part, I should not pine much if both were forgot."

Nevertheless if either wife Martha's parrot or granddaughter Nellie's dog had been left behind, the first to set out to retrace his steps and find them would have been the Father of his Country.

## 2: MR. JEFFERSON'S MOCKINGBIRD

Mockingbirds sang in the wooded hills of Albemarle County, Virginia, when Thomas Jefferson was a little boy, and he never forgot their ecstatic music sounding through the soft Virginia air—not even when he became the third President of the United States. After he had written the immortal Declaration of Independence and after the War for Independence had been won, he was appointed to represent the new nation, the United States of America, in France, the beautiful and friendly land that had generously aided the Continental Army in its long struggle for freedom. Even there, however, in the loveliest of French landscapes, his thoughts were of the beauties of his homeland.

Mr. Jefferson broke his right wrist in the autumn of 1786. The bones did not heal well and gave him great pain. In the spring of the next year, he set out on a journey through the south of France in the hope that the warm waters that welled from the earth there might hasten his recovery. It so happened that at an hour late in May, while General George Washington, Benjamin Franklin, John Adams, Alexander Hamilton, James Madison and many

other great Americans were meeting in Philadelphia to create a constitution which would bind the thirteen states into a unified nation, Thomas Jefferson was traveling the clear still waters of a quiet French canal. While the horses ahead of his boat plodded along the towpath, drawing the craft on its way, the tall red-haired, young-looking man was writing slowly and painfully, because his wrist still bothered him, a letter to his elder daughter, fifteen-year-old Martha, to whom he had given the nickname "Patsy."

As he wrote, the blue of the sky was reflected in the mirror of the waters below, and from the Lombardy poplars and the drooping willows that lined the canal came bursts of lovely bird song. As if arranged in rows like a large choir, the nightingales of southern France, most delightful of all European bird singers, were warbling their joy in a perfect sunlit moment of the spring. As he listened, enchanted, it seemed as if he were drifting down a watery aisle of song.

Mr. Jefferson was so moved by what he saw and heard that he described the scene to Patsy, who was a student in a convent school in Paris. He said that once before in his life and in this same country he had heard a matchless concert from the throats of nightingales. This had been, he wrote, near the charming old French town of Avignon, at a spot where a fountain "of the size of a river" gushed from a narrow valley between high mountains. Above him, at that time, he could see at the top of a steep hill the ruins of an ancient dwelling. "Every tree and bush," he wrote, "was filled with nightingales in full song."

When Patsy received this letter, she read: "As you have trees in the garden of the convent there might be nightingales in them, and this is the season of their song." Then her devoted father, ever mindful of his loved Virginia home, wrote, "Endeavor, my dear, to make yourself acquainted with the music of this bird, that when you return to your own country you may be able to estimate its merit in comparison with that of the mocking-bird."

Five years later, when Patsy had become the wife of Mr. Thomas Randolph, and later a proud mother, she wrote to her father that she and her children had witnessed the arrival of a mockingbird near their home.

Mr. Jefferson was then American Secretary of State. Since Philadelphia was the national capital, he had rented for the hot summer months a residence on the banks of the nearby Schuylkill River. Here it was his custom to write his letters outdoors in the shade of high plane trees. De-

lighted with his daughter's report, he wrote that he longed
for the day to come when his own home, Monticello, might
also have high trees about it where birds might nest. Then
he wrote her: "I sincerely congratulate you on the arrival of
the mocking-bird" and said he hoped she would teach her
children to respect the newcomer as "a superior being in
the form of a bird." He added that she should tell the children stories that people often tell about mockingbirds.
One of these was that if anybody killed one or stole its
eggs, the bird would haunt him for years to come. Perhaps
he was thinking, too, of a superstition many Virginians still
relate—that if an unmarried girl will put on a man's hat
during the midnight song of a mockingbird, her wedding
will take place before the end of the year.

These examples of Mr. Jefferson's affection for the song-
birds that had filled the Virginia meadows and groves with
melodies during his boyhood make less surprising the fact
that after he had been elected President of the United States
in 1801 and had entered the unfinished President's House,
a tamed mockingbird became his favorite indoor companion. Since his beloved wife had died when his own children
were very young, and since neither they nor his grandchildren could come to live with him in the big stone mansion
in Washington, the bird that sang for him received much of
his grateful attention and love.

The President's private office, which he called his "cabinet," was on the basement or ground floor of the house.
Its walls were covered with maps, bookcases, and other
proofs of his interest in the whole wide world. A long table

stood in the middle of the room, and drawers on either side of it held his set of carpenter's tools and his small garden tools. In the light that streamed through his windows lay his indoor garden of plants and flowers, and he liked puttering about them, watering them and loosening the soil at their roots.

In this bower that held roses and geraniums hung the cage of his slim gray bird. Often when no one else was with him he would open the little barred door and the mocker would hop out. The two white chevrons on each of its gray wings and the white of its tail feathers gleamed

brightly as it swooped about, exploring the room with a
never-satisfied curiosity. Sometimes the President would
place a cherry or other bit of fruit between his lips and
the bird, perching upon his shoulder, would make delighted stabs at it with its beak. When it was no longer
hungry it would drop down to the surface of the table and,
using that as a concert stage, it would sing for its audience
of one an ever-changing concert, interrupting its loveliest
melodies with funny imitations of the barking of a dog, the
mewing of a cat, the sharp warning call of a robin.

Often, too, when the President was weary of the duties
of his office, he would go to his chamber above to rest and
the bird would follow him. As Mr. Jefferson climbed the
stairs, his little gray friend, choosing not to fly, would hop
up each step, facing now to the left and now to the right,
and flirting its tail to show the pure white lining. Then,
as the tall man reclined on his couch, worried by some of
the most difficult problems that this nation has ever faced,
the mocker, perched beside him, would sing and sing until
the furrows on his hearer's brow disappeared and the President of the United States had fallen into a deep, untroubled
sleep. It may seem a little silly to try to measure what effect
the gray bird had on our nation's history, nevertheless we
know that a mockingbird gave to a great President recreation and rest at a time when they were necessary to his
doing well the tremendous tasks that were his to do.

## 3:  DOLLEY MADISON'S MACAW

Dolley, the pretty young wife of James Madison, fourth President of our nation, knew Thomas Jefferson's mockingbird quite well. Mr. Jefferson, who had appointed her husband his Secretary of State, often asked Dolley to help him welcome guests to his dinners and other parties at the President's House, and so she was accustomed to hearing and seeing the gray singer in his cage among the green vines and plants.

Dolley's choice of a pet, however, was more in keeping with her own exciting and colorful self. Mr. Jefferson's bird wore gray with trimmings of white, the sort of modest colors that Dolley's Quaker parents were accustomed to wear. When she was young, however, Dolley had seen a macaw and the brilliant blue and gold and red of the bird pleased her so much that she begged her father and mother to buy her one of these gaudy South American creatures. Patiently it was explained to her that Quakers wore only dull colors and spoke only in quiet tones. It would be unseemly, said her mother, for a daughter of hers to own a bird of such strong colors and such a loud and unmusical voice.

Nevertheless, by the time Dolley had married Mr. Madi-

son and become the First Lady of the land, she owned a
macaw and had spent many hours teaching it to talk. When
she gave parties at the President's House, it was really hard
to tell whether she or the parrot was the gayer sight, for
Dolley loved to dress in gowns of bright colors. It can safely
be said that the President's wife was the more polite to her
guests, for her parrot used to scream at them when they

gathered about its cage; and if it said, "Polly wants a cracker," it said the words so loudly that they could be heard throughout the whole big house.

During the War of 1812 the British Fleet anchored in Chesapeake Bay and stayed there for more than a year. Admiral Cockburn, the Fleet Commander, sent Dolley Madison the insolent message that he would soon enter her drawing room. In mid-August of 1814, at the head of a large force, he set out to make good his word. American forces, hastily gathered to meet the invasion, were defeated at Bladensburg on August 24, and Washington lay helpless before the advancing enemy.

The city so threatened was at first noisy and turbulent as many of its people who chose to leave packed belongings into their wagons and urged their horses into the crowded highways leading north. Then came a dead silence. The streets of the capital were deserted. All that week the weather had been mercilessly hot, and although rain had seemed about to pour from overhanging dark clouds, not a drop had fallen. Lightning flashed along the horizon and thunder muttered briefly. Somewhere to the south, the people of Washington knew, an army of redcoats was marching toward them, and there could be no resistance.

While the cannonading went on at Bladensburg Dolley Madison sat alone at her desk in the President's House. Her husband had left to join the American forces. John Sioussat, the loyal French-born head of her staff of servants, stood beside her.

"French John," she wrote (using his familiar nickname)

". . . offers to spike the cannon at the gates, and to lay a train of powder which would blow up the British should they enter the house." After persuading the enterprising fellow not to try this stratagem, Dolley went to bed and on the next day, August 24, was so busy that she could not continue her letter until noon. She told her sister she was removing the big portrait of General Washington, painted by the famous painter, Gilbert Stuart, from the wall where it hung, in order to save it.

"And now, dear sister, I must leave this house or the retreating army will make me a prisoner in it by filling up the road I am directed to take. When I shall see or write you, or where I shall be tomorrow, I cannot tell!"

Soon after Dolley Madison had left the house, all the servants of the President's House who had not already departed, fled from it with the single exception of French John. He still had one duty he was determined to perform. From among the plants and vines of Mrs. Madison's sitting room sounded a voice, a familiar fearless screech. To the cage hung in the greenery French John marched and, lifting it from its hook, lowered it and its occupant. He turned then and carried his burden into the great hall leading to the front door. Through the long passage shadowed by a forest of wide pillars he stepped, and the cries of the aroused bird echoed weirdly through the emptiness of the big house. The huge lamps that had once illuminated gay assemblies here were unlighted now and the front door opened on gathering dusk.

Down the steps strode French John, the cage bumping

at his side, the macaw shrilly protesting its unaccustomed ride. While the tread of the British troops resounded through the lonely streets the loyal servant was making his way to the only safety that he knew—to Octagon House, winter home of Mr. Benjamin Tayloe, but now the temporary residence of the French Minister to the United States, Monsieur Sérurier. To his fellow-countrymen's care, French John delivered Dolley Madison's precious talking bird. Even as he did so, flames from the President's House were licking up into the dark sky behind him. The fires set by the British throughout the city were so hot that even the wild downpour of rain that evening did not put them out. All night lightning flashed and thunder rolled above the city.

The macaw was soon moved again, for Mr. Madison and his wife in a few months went to Octagon House to live while the President's ruined dwelling was being redesigned and rebuilt. (When this work had been accomplished, it was painted a gleaming white and thus came to be known as "the White House.")

Meanwhile the Madisons moved again within the year, this time to a simple and modest home at the corner of Pennsylvania Avenue and Nineteenth Street in Washington. The walls of this house bordered the street, and children coming home from school could sometimes see Dolley Madison feeding her macaw in its cage by one of the windows. When the President's wife saw the boys and girls watching her she would open the window and, placing the cage in it, would persuade the bird to perform its tricks for them and talk to them. It would be hard to say who got the most fun out of these little shows—the children, Dolley Madison, or the bird.

Both the parrot and its owner lived many years. After his two terms as President, Mr. Madison and his wife returned to the old Madison home in Orange County, Virginia, and of course the bird went with them. It was still very much alive after Mr. Madison died in 1836, and it was still an object of amusement and affection in Dolley Madison's seventieth year. Whether the macaw lived on after Dolley's death at the age of eighty-one is not, so far as I know, recorded.

## 4: ZACK TAYLOR'S OLD WHITEY

Old Whitey was the most popular horse in America long before he began nibbling the grass on the White House lawn. In the spring of 1846, when the war with Mexico was at its height, all dispatches from the advancing army of the United States told of a strange and valiant pair —a white horse and an old general—who won much of the credit for a series of American victories. Old Whitey, they said, looked more like a carriage horse than a battle charger. The old man, officially known as General Zachary Taylor but called by thousands of his admiring troops "Old Zack," "Old Rough and Ready," or just simply "the Old Man," looked more like a farmer than the heroic general that he was.

Old Whitey was big and square, and although slightly knock-kneed, he was well proportioned. His grayish white coat was rough and uneven, his mane shaggy, his tail long and coarse.

Old Zack, like his horse, had little military bearing. His uniform was never "regulation" and frequently was outlandish. His subordinate officers, who loved and respected him, once guessed that aside from his floppy straw hat with a brim so broad it shaded his whole stout body, his uniform had cost him seven and a half dollars. A shapeless green coat fitted loosely on his heavy long-armed body; and light-blue britches, unpressed and worn, covered his short legs and were tucked carelessly into the gaping tops of wrinkled army boots. His face was seamed and sunburned and his hair was gray. Reporters almost always described his hazel eyes whose piercing eagle-like look could quickly become warm and friendly. His nose was long and his mouth was thin, sometimes resolute and stubborn, sometimes humorous and smiling. He was incredibly brave. He never ordered his men into dangers he would not risk himself. Old Whitey, like his master, was equally fearless on the battlefield, indifferent to the deafening roar of cannons, the red glare of bursting shells and the whining of bullets.

At the Texas town of Palo Alto, the Americans found the enemy blocking their advance. General Taylor, astride Old Whitey, drew his sword and led his men to battle. Though burning gun wads set the mesquite and chaparral afire and dense smoke hid the fighters from each other, the men could see the white horse constantly in front carrying his master as calmly as though he were leading a march. All day, steadfast, he moved back and forth before the American lines. As darkness fell the enemy withdrew and Old Zack gave the order to bivouac on the field. Horses and men alike were exhausted. Old Whitey rested near his master. The night air was cool and pleasant to him after the long, hot day. No gunfire broke the stillness of the star-

filled night. In the early morning, however, the Mexicans returned to the fray. Under the eyes of Old Zack and his white horse, the Americans, whooping and yelling, stormed ahead and drove the enemy from the field.

When news of this victory reached the grateful people of the United States, the fame of Old Whitey and the Old Man spread rapidly, and the modest pair became great heroes. Men enlisted by the thousands to serve under the great general. During the long, hot summer months Old Whitey went on long marches. He stood by patiently while the new artillerymen learned to shoot the big cannons on the range. In camp he was tethered outside Old Zack's tent where he nibbled grass and showed great interest in all who came to see the general. Old Whitey was a great favorite with the men, and they often brought him bits of sugar or an apple, and he nuzzled them to show his appreciation. Whenever the men drilled to the music of the military bands and Old Zack rode him at the head of the marching column, the horse pricked up his ears and pranced because, of all things in the world, he most loved a parade.

The day finally came when the small army was ready to set out for their objective—the city of Monterey, three hundred miles from their camp. Old Whitey and Old Rough and Ready traveled with the troops, sharing the hardships of the difficult trek. Days were unbearably hot; nights often so cold that campfires were needed. On the rough, narrow, mountainous roads Old Whitey sometimes helped pull the big guns up steep inclines. Sometimes he carried Old Zack to the rear of the long columns while the Old Man in his ragged straw hat advised on the moving of the clumsy supply wagons. And each time the men saw these two their spirits rose and their affection grew deeper.

After several weeks the army reached a beautiful plain. There, in a shady grove, they pitched their tents. Upon entering this lovely spot, Old Whitey, hot and tired, went at once to drink from one of the many crystal-clear springs that flowed from gentle slopes. Old Zack dismounted and, removing his straw hat, bathed his sunburned face in the cooling waters. Then he dipped a rag into the spring and wiped the sweat off Old Whitey's face and neck. This was indeed a pleasant spot. Then refreshed, Old Zack remounted and rode Old Whitey to the edge of the grove. Standing on the summit of a small hill, the two could see before them the shining city of Monterey.

They could hear bells ringing, the continous roll of drums and the blare of bugles. They could see the red, white and green of the Mexican flag flying above one of the high towers of the cathedral. Pennons floated above the dark walls of the citadel. The sounds and the colors excited Old Whitey. He arched his neck and he made little dancing steps, expecting, no doubt, that there would be a parade. At that moment a cannon roared and the shot fell just ten feet away from him. He seemed to sigh with disappointment. Soon the air was filled with smoke and fire and the constant roar of the guns. In the midst of flying bullets and the turmoil of battle Old Whitey carried his master, and at every opportunity he lowered his head to taste the grass beneath his feet.

As parts of the city fell into American hands, Old Rough and Ready dismounted to fight beside his men in hand-to-hand struggles in the streets. Old Whitey followed his master as closely as he could. When the Mexican flag was lowered from the cathedral and the Stars and Stripes took its place, he walked behind Old Zack, who ambled toward the cheering men, though Mexican bullets were falling like hickory nuts all around them.

For three days and three nights the fighting continued but at last the city fell and the Mexican army withdrew. When Old Whitey heard the Yanks shouting with joy and heard the band strike up, he forgot he was tired and pawed the ground impatiently. To the tune of "Yankee Doodle," with Old Zack on his back, he led the conquering heroes into the city. In front of the cathedral they pulled out of line to stand as the troops passed in review before them. Swinging his great old head and occasionally snorting his pleasure, Old Whitey watched as first the Phoenix Company, each man dressed as he pleased, in a red shirt, in a blue shirt, in a brown shirt, but looking sure and seasoned, went by. Next came the artillerymen in dark blue with red stripes on their pants. The infantry in pale blue followed them. Old Whitey whinnied as though he were cheering when the Rangers passed in fringed leggings and buckskin caps, armed with rifles and bowie knives, and he stood still as if at attention when the regulars trooped in front of him.

The following weeks went by without excitement for Old Whitey. When Old Zack did not need him, he grazed. He liked being among the men who made a great pet of

him. He was curious about their activities, sometimes
shoving his way into a group of them. And the men always
laughed and slapped his haunches affectionately. He was a
privileged character.

One day he noticed that the army was ready to move.
He watched them depart but he and Old Zack did not go
along. In a few days, though, they too left the camp. They
rode through mountainous country filled with ravines so
deep as to be almost impassable. They crossed arid, cactus-
dotted plains. Under blazing sun and through heavy rain-
falls they rode to Buena Vista. The sounds of gunfire
reached their ears before the white horse and his rider
could see the troops they had come to join. Hurriedly
ascending a ridge, they saw before them on a high plateau
the American soldiers retreating in great disorder before
the resplendently uniformed Mexican troops. In formation
the enemy rode toward the hill, their gold braid catching
the light, their plumes blowing and their pennons flying,
and the tips of their lances gleaming in the sunlight.

When the Americans soldiers suddenly saw Old Whitey
appear on the top of the hill, when they saw the slouching
confident figure of the Old Man on his back, a great cheer
went up and the men turned with renewed courage upon
the advancing foe. Old Zack quietly gave a command to
the officer near him. "Give them a little more grape, Mr.
Bragg," he said to the general in command of the artillery,
"That's the way to do it."

All through the battle Old Whitey nibbled grass while
Old Zack, one leg thrown over the pommel of the saddle,

took notes and gave his orders. Unperturbed by flying bullets, though one ripped across his chest and another tore through his sleeve, the general stayed on the hill, although he and the white horse under him made a perfect target for the enemy. By late afternoon the Americans had again routed the foe.

The news of this victory was received in the United States with great joy. After two years in Mexico, General Taylor was given a well-earned leave. Amid sorrowful goodbys the two warriors—the old general and the white horse —boarded the ship *Monmouth* and set sail for home. Thirteen vessels were waiting at the mouth of the Mississippi River to escort them to New Orleans where a great celebration was prepared. Old Whitey, saddled for the first time in many days, stood beside the general on the deck. A hundred guns saluted as they landed and the spectators were delighted to see the eager horse so interested in everything.

Old Zack and Old Whitey were led through a triumphal arch of evergreens when they came ashore at Jackson Square. Then the cheering throngs became quiet as the campaigners stood silently to hear the *Te Deum* sung in the cathedral. Flags and banners floated in the soft air, and when the Old Man mounted his horse the crowds again cheered loudly. Old Whitey, hearing the military band strike up a march, pranced about, impatient for the great parade to get underway. Then, leading a long procession, he proudly bore his master through the streets. Spectators threw flowers in their path as they made their way to the St. Charles Hotel where a splendid banquet had been prepared.

The next day, once more afloat on the Mississippi, horse and man began their journey to their home in Baton Rouge, Louisiana. Along the way cannons roared a welcome and hundreds of flags waved above the levees. Bands played on passing steamboats. Old Whitey stood nodding his head and pawing the deck in delight. After they had reached Baton Rouge, the old general rode the horse slowly and comfortably all the distance to his plantation, Cypress Grove.

Old Whitey spent the next months restfully at his master's home high on the bank of the Mississippi. He grazed peacefully on the tree-shaded lawn while the Old Man rocked on the vine-covered porch. Once in a while he carried his master down to the boat landing to greet visitors. It was a quiet pleasant time.

With the coming of summer Whitey saw more guests than usual coming to Cypress Grove. In the autumn his master was away frequently and the horse missed his daily attentions. He could not know that his old friend would soon become the President of the United States.

In February of the year 1849 Old Whitey was aware of great activity all about him. People moved faster than usual, lights in the house sometimes burned all night long, fires flared more often on the river's bank. Then one day he was led aboard a steamboat to begin the long journey to his new home, in Washington.

When he arrived, Old Whitey was put to pasture on the

green lawn of the White House. Here he roamed at will. Though Senator William Seward of New York had given him, through his master, a silver-toothed currycomb his coat remained as shaggy as ever. The famous horse delighted in the attentions he received from visitors. When he stood at the fence bordering the lawn, no one passed by without stopping to say a word to him and to pat his head. Frequently he found his beloved master walking among the crowds on the lawn of the White House.

One April afternoon when he was nibbling grass in a corner of the lawn, the Phoenix Hook and Ladder Company of New York City, on a visit to Washington firemen, came to see the President. They were escorted by their hosts to the White House and, upon entering the grounds, their band struck up a tune. Old Whitey pricked up his ears, turned, and seeing the red jackets and blue pants of the marching firemen, galloped toward them, so happy was he to hear the military music and so eager to be in the parade. The firemen lost step as he dashed among them seeking his accustomed place behind the standard bearers, and the band, laughing and in great confusion, had difficulty in playing their instruments. The spectators howled in merriment, and those who looked out of the windows of the White House saw Old Whitey with arched neck and high-lifted hoofs once more "showing off" in a parade.

One day a gentleman so elegantly dressed that he was considered a famous dude paid a call on Old Whitey. He was Nathaniel Parker Willis, one of America's most widely known poets and the editor of the *Home Journal* (later the

*Ladies Home Journal*). Mr. Willis wrote a description of his visit:

"We felt the smoke of Buena Vista . . . , of Palo Alto and Monterey, pushing us toward the cannon-proof old charger. He went smelling about the edges of the sidewalk . . . and we crossed over to have a nearer look at him, with a feeling that the glory was not all taken from his back with the saddle and holsters. . . . He had evidently been long untouched by a curry-comb—the name of 'Old Whitey,' indeed, hardly describing with fidelity a coat so matted and yellow. But remembering the beatings of the great heart that he had borne upon his back—the anxieties, the energies, the defiances of danger . . . it was impossible to look upon him without a throb in the throat. . . ."

On Saturday afternoons Old Whitey was tethered to a tree during the Marine concerts on the White House lawn. He pawed the ground and tossed his head when the music played. At the end of the concert he waited patiently for his master who, dressed in a loose-fitting black broadcloth suit, a tall silk hat on the back of his head in place of the old floppy straw, walked among the crowds chatting with everyone. He knew the Old Man would not leave without speaking to him and giving him an affectionate slap. These were happy days for Old Whitey.

As his second summer in Washington approached, the heat became intense and the horse listlessly sought the shade under the trees on the lawn. His master took a short vacation and when he returned in the beginning of July he was very ill. Old Whitey did not know this but he was

aware that the many visitors to the White House were no
longer the gay crowds he was so fond of. These visitors were
solemn people and seemed not to have time for the friendly
words they usually had for the old horse. He missed his
master and wandered around as near to the White House
as he could. On July 9, 1850, Old Whitey heard the tolling
of a great bell and the answering peals from the spires of
Washington's churches. Old Rough and Ready, the fearless
old general, the beloved President of the United States, was
dead.

For three days Old Whitey saw thousands of grieving
people dressed in black and with bowed heads, go in and
out of the White House. On the morning of the fourth day,
a groom led him to the stable. While the man combed his
matted yellowed coat and untangled the snarls in his mane
with the silver currycomb, he stood patiently, knowing that
this was a special occasion. He was harnessed and the saddle
was once more placed on his back. His master's empty
boots, reversed, were fitted into the stirrups. Then the
old war horse was led out to take his place in the long
procession honoring the memory of the Old Man.

General Winfield Scott, yellow plumes waving from his
high helmet, rode on a spirited charger at the head of the
artillery companies, veterans of the Mexican War. The
coffin, under a canopy draped in black and surmounted by
a golden eagle, lay on the funeral carriage which was
drawn by eight white horses, each led by a Negro dressed
in white. Immediately behind, Old Whitey walked alone.
More troops followed him. Bells tolled and cannons

boomed. Spectators, lining the streets through which the sorrowing columns passed quietly, wept when they saw Old Whitey walking slowly, his saddle empty, his head bowed. He seemed to know that this was the last parade.

## 5: FATHER ABRAHAM AND THE GOAT TEAM

The White House was in an uproar. The servants ran about carrying large pans of water and stacks of blankets. Some of them went down to the kitchens and some scurried out to the stable. Tad and Willie stood wide-eyed and flushed, having been scolded by their mother several times. They waited impatiently in the corridor for news. Then the door of the kitchen flew open and Abraham Lincoln, sixteenth President of the United States, announced to his sons with great joy that Tad's dog had just borne a litter of pups.

"The prettiest pups you ever did see," said Mr. Lincoln. At that very moment Mrs. Lincoln ran in from the stable calling out that Tabby, Willie's cat, had given birth to the "cutest batch of kittens the White House would ever see."

Mr. Lincoln was as excited as his youngsters about the new additions to the White House. His wife had as much difficulty in quieting her husband as she had in calming her sons. That day, and for many days after the happy event, the President showed his excitement by announcing the news to senators, generals and foreign and domestic men of importance as they called at the White House on

matters of state. When the boys consulted him in the
matter of naming the new pets he gave the problem grave
consideration.

When Abraham Lincoln had been a little boy himself, his
father had struggled desperately to earn enough to feed
his family. Many times the weather was unkind and rains
and floods washed away seeds that had held promise for
a good crop. As a child young Abe had yearned for a pony
of his own, but knowing how scarce food was, he never
asked.

Later, when Mr. Lincoln was a struggling young lawyer
in Illinois, he was riding in a stage one day on his way to
visit a client who lived on a small farm. As the coach rum-
bled past a ditch which was filled with mud, the pas-
sengers noticed a little pig stuck fast in the muck, struggling to free itself and squealing furiously. Everyone
laughed but Mr. Lincoln, who could see nothing funny
in the pig's sad plight. He asked the driver to stop and
amid the snickers of the others stepped ankle-deep into
the mud. Carefully he picked the animal up and set it
on solid ground. When he returned to the stage his only
suit was covered with dirt, but his heart was too full of the
satisfaction of having done a good deed for him to notice it.

Now that he had children of his own who shared his
deep love for animals, it was Mr. Lincoln's pleasure to let
them have as many pets as they wished.

Most loved of all were two ponies in the Presidential
stable. These had been promised to Willie and Tad by their
indulgent parents as consolation for leaving their shaggy

brown dog, Fido, in Springfield when the family set out
for Washington. Mr. Lincoln had pointed out, reasonably
as always, that there were two reasons why Fido must be
left behind. "For one thing your mother has her hands full
enough packing us off to the White House to care much
about adding a dog to the party," he said. "For another
thing, Fido is only half ours, and I don't know that we
could agree on which half our family is entitled to take."

The boys had admitted the reasons were sound. Mary
Lincoln was an adoring mother, but her temper could be
sharp, particularly when she was tired, and the boys had
learned, quite as well as their father, that it wasn't wise
to "stir Mother up." Fido *was* only half their pet, for he
belonged equally to the Roll boys who lived down the
street and were the Lincoln boys' best friends. The dog
had trotted amiably back and forth between the two houses
ever since puppyhood, often getting double meals as a
result. Nevertheless, though Mrs. Lincoln took time from
her packing on their last day in Springfield to have a keep-
sake photograph made of Fido in the company of Willie
and Tad, the boys had raised such a dismal howl on the
way to the Springfield depot that Mr. Lincoln, quite possibly in desperation, had promised they should have ponies
of their own as soon as they reached Washington if they
would "be good boys and not bother Mother on the journey."

The promise was kept and two lively ponies were
promptly installed in the White House stables. Willie and
Tad were delighted. Every fine morning they would gallop

along the avenues of the capital. Mr. Lincoln on his own horse was not far behind, long legs dangling from his saddle, stovepipe hat perched atop his head, eyes twinkling proudly at his sons.

In spite of the shadow of war under which the Lincolns lived in Washington, and the lines of sorrow and weariness that grew deeper in Mr. Lincoln's face as, month after month, he studied battle reports, often until late at night waiting for the endless lists of casualties, the family, especially the two boys, could still be happy. So long as Willie and Tad were about, their liveliness—even their mischief—seldom failed to bring an indulgent smile from their mother and to lighten their father's tired eyes with laughter.

The Lincolns had lived in the White House little more than a year, however, when Willie Lincoln fell ill. In spite of everything the doctors could do, in spite of mother's nursing and the hours when his father left his office to sit patiently beside the boy's bed, Willie died.

Tad was desolate, for the brothers had been inseparable. In Springfield there had been other playmates. Washington, however, was very different. Children of the President of the United States were not expected to roam about making neighborhood friends, and for nine-year-old Taddie, left alone, the White House became a dreary place.

Some time after Willie's death, an alarm woke the household one night. There was a fire in the stables. First to rush to the rescue was Mr. Lincoln, and it took the White House guards to force the President to come back into the White House. There was always the danger, their frightened captain explained, that the fire might have been set purposely just to coax the President out into the night in order to give an assassin the chance to attack him. Mr. Lincoln only shook his head. Willie's pony, which the boy had dearly loved, was still in the burning stable. Willie's father had meant to save it.

Without Willie, even the joy of his own pony was lost for Tad. When the President asked why he never rode any more, Tad replied, "The ponies make me miss Willie even more."

A new gift of pets arrived in the early spring, when a kind gentleman from Philadelphia sent a pair of white rabbits to "Master Tad Lincoln." The rabbits had pink eyes and quivering noses and Tad enjoyed stroking their velvety soft fur. Mr. Lincoln wrote gratefully to the sender:

Executive Mansion
April 2, 1862

Dear Sir

Allow me to thank you in behalf of my little son for your present of White Rabbits. He is very much pleased with them.

Yours truly,
Abraham Lincoln

The gayest pets the White House ever saw came soon after. They were a pair of goats. William H. Tisdale, an orderly to Mr. Lincoln, vividly recalled the story of these lively young creatures.

One day when the President, Mrs. Lincoln and Tad were driving out toward the Navy Yard, Mr. Tisdale wrote, they spied several goats busily chewing grass and shrubs. All the families in that neighborhood owned goats which, besides giving milk, were also the family pets. For the first time since Willie died, Tad's eyes lighted up.

When Mr. Lincoln and his family returned home, he said to Mr. Tisdale, "Go down tomorrow and see if you can buy me a pair of goats." The orderly went directly to the families near the Navy Yard, offering to buy what the President had ordered. Finally he found just what he was sure the President would want, a healthy pair of half-grown goats. "They were willing to sell them for five dollars each," Mr. Tisdale said, "and since they were well matched, I bought them."

The President purchased a strong wagon and had the saddler make a pair of harnesses. "Then," as Mr. Tisdale remembered it, "the fun began." It took a little time and a lot of patience for the goats to be broken to harness so that Tad could drive them safely, but it was worth all the trouble. Mr. Lincoln, when he watched the goats and the smiling boy, looked very much like a man without a worry in the world. When the goats would hop up and down he would throw back his head and laugh like a schoolboy.

All the youngsters in the neighborhood and many of the children belonging to the President's staff joined Tad and his new pets on the White House grounds. The boys and

girls took turns riding in the wagon and each time the
goats stopped to admire the grass the children screamed

with laughter. Mrs. Lincoln, in spite of being a very particular housekeeper, seemed to welcome all the dogs and cats that wandered constantly in and out of the house. But she rebelled the day the goats came into the kitchen looking, she thought, for a change of diet. It was only when Mr. Lincoln came back to the kitchen, laughing so hard he had to use a kerchief to muffle the sounds, that his wife learned the real reason for the goats' presence.

A group of distinguished Boston ladies had been viewing the east room of the executive mansion only a few minutes before when young Tad came storming through the room behind two goats, one harnessed in front of the other and dragging a chariot consisting of a kitchen chair. So far as Mr. Lincoln was concerned his beloved Tad could do no wrong, but the ladies from Boston made it quite clear they would much prefer the goats elsewhere.

It was the President's duty, according to Tad, to take care of the goats when he and his mother went on short vacations. On one of these trips Mrs. Lincoln received a telegram from her husband saying, "Tell Tad the goats and father are very well, especially the goats."

But once while Tad and his mother were visiting relatives Mrs. Lincoln received a telegram that upset everyone including the telegraph office. It let Tad know that one of the goats, Nanko, had left home. She had been sitting prettily in the middle of Tad's bed, happily chewing her cud, but after having been ordered out of the room she wandered into the garden and proceeded to eat the flowers. The gardener chased her away several times and suggested

Nanny be moved to another part of the White House grounds. Somehow then she disappeared. The President ventured to make the guess that Nanny had been insulted once too often and had left in a goatish huff.

Mr. Noah Brooks, a newspaper correspondent of whom Mr. Lincoln was very fond, wrote a little story about another of Tad's pets—Jack, the turkey. Jack had been intended for the family Thanksgiving dinner in 1863 but Tad had taken such a fancy to the bird and pleaded so pathetically for his life that the President allowed him to live on as a White House pet.

Election Day of 1864 was gloomy, and the dark clouds poured down a heavy rain on Washington. Since the soldiers stationed in Washington could not go home to vote, some of the states had sent commissions to Washington to set up voting facilities for these absentees. Pennsylvania had sent such a commission, and a regiment of "bucktails" as these men were called were voting on the lawn of the White House. Tad had seen them there and he ran into the office where Mr. Lincoln and Noah Brooks were sitting, begging his father to come to the window that he might see all the uniformed men "voting for Lincoln and Johnson." Looking out, the President saw not only the line of voters but Jack, the turkey, strutting among them in an interested way.

"What business has your turkey stalking about the voting polls in that way?" Mr. Lincoln asked his son. "Does he vote?"

"No," said Tad, "he is not of age."

Mr. Brooks and Mr. Lincoln laughed long and loud over the little boy's quick answer and the President, in the days that followed, often told the story with pride.

It is natural for men to love tame animals and Abraham Lincoln, one of the kindest and most humane of all of America's presidents, had a real affection for them. That they, in turn, relieved and diverted him when his mind was heavy with the troubles and griefs brought on by civil war, cannot be doubted.

## 6:   PRESIDENT GRANT AND BUTCHER'S BOY

President Ulysses Simpson Grant was brought up on a farm and had known and understood farm animals almost from the time of his birth. There seemed to be an unusual relationship between the boy and horses. It was almost as if they communicated with each other in a secret and silent language. By the time young Grant had graduated at West Point in 1843 he was one of the best of horsemen. Stories of his astonishing feats of riding came out of the Mexican War and later out of the Civil War.

It is not surprising then that when the Grants lived at the White House new stables were built with stalls for many horses. The first pets to be noted by the President, however, were not horses but canaries. A big building had been put up on Judiciary Square in Washington for the express purpose of housing the ball which was to follow the President's inauguration ceremony. The main ballroom was three hundred feet long and a hundred and fifty feet wide. The hastily built wooden walls had been draped with a white cloth and the effect was so beautiful that the room immediately won a name—"The Muslin Palace." At the center, the highest point, hung a magnificent wooden American eagle, holding in its talons the shield of the United States. From this, red, white and blue streamers were strung to every part of the hall, each one ending in a representation of the coat of arms of one of the states. Behind the platform on which the President and his party would be received, a series of gaslights, arranged to look like a brilliant sunrise, lighted the whole ballroom.

It had been planned that while the nation's Chief Executive and his companions were entering, the Marine Band would be playing "Hail to the Chief." When Mr. Grant had reached the platform the band brasses would cease and then, from cages cleverly hung from the ceiling, hundreds of canaries would be singing their hearts out in a rapturous greeting to the new President.

On March fourth of 1869, unfortunately the weather had not collaborated with the committee for the ball. Those who witnessed the inauguration had stood shivering in a freezing temperature. And when the Marine Band's crashing march had suddenly ended and it was time for the canaries to pour out their ecstatic songs—not one offered even a peep. All of them had tucked their heads under their wings and were much too cold to sing a note.

Throughout his eight years at the White House Mr. Grant took great joy in his horses. Every day he strolled down to the stables to stroke their silky coats and say a word or two to each one. Little black Jeff Davis, so spirited as to be almost unmanageable and given his name for that very reason, had been his battle mount when he had been the general in command of the Union forces and the horse was still

a favorite. Cincinnatus, a dark bay, was his more depend-
able saddle horse. Never alarmed by brass bands, cannon or
unexpected events, he would wait even for hours at a
stretch, without being tied, whenever his master left him.
Egypt and St. Louis were a perfectly matched team for the
President when he wished to take his wife or honored guests

to see Washington and its surroundings. Two Shetland ponies, Red and Billy Button, were for the delight of the young sons, Buck (Ulysses Junior) and Jesse, who were driven to school through the White House grounds and the Washington streets (as fast as they could get their driver to go) in a little wagon exactly suited to the size of both steeds and their masters. Nellie, who was older than her brothers, owned the mares Jennie and Mary, somewhat more sedate than their stable companions.

Lastly there was Julia, the buggy horse. She was a fast-stepping racer and the buggy was a light racing rig. On many a sunny afternoon, Mr. Grant would leave the cares of his office behind, and set out along the Washington streets as if he were going for a quiet drive. At these times he was not easily recognizable because he used to pull the wide brim of his hat down until his eyes could hardly be seen, and bend over the dashboard until his shoulders were almost touching it. Thus disguised, the President of the United States would look about for competition—and this was not usually lacking. Having picked a horse that was fast and a driver who seemed proud of the fact, Mr. Grant would, upon seeing a level stretch of road, drive up even with his chosen rival in an obvious challenge that was hardly ever refused. In a split second the hooves of both horses would be drumming a wild tattoo on the soft smooth road. As they neared the end of the stretch the President would speak softly to his horse and the flying animal would put on a burst of speed that would leave the driver of the other rig choking on the dust from victorious hooves.

There was a day, however, when the President got more competition than he bargained for. He had casually pulled out to pass a boy driving a delivery wagon when he was surprised to notice that he was not passing. On the contrary, the wagon seemed to be moving ahead of his racing buggy. Off they went—the President in his racing rig and the delivery boy in his wagon. No amount of speaking to his horse helped the President that day. The boy stayed

ahead until he had to slow up at the butcher shop where he worked. Mr. Grant turned about after the match was over and made sure of the address of that butcher's shop.

A few days later a representative of the President called at the shop on a matter of business. The meat which he bought that day was live and very literally "on the hoof." In the White House stables a new name was being painted on one of the stalls. There—beside such highfaluting names as Jeff Davis and Cincinnatus and Egypt and St. Louis—was a more homely title. It read "Butcher's Boy" and often thereafter when Mr. Grant went out for a drive and looked for opposition, the horse furiously setting the pace that put his master out ahead of his rivals was the one which, driven by a delivery boy, had made the President of the United States eat his dust.

## 7:  THE  MERRY  MENAGERIE

The White House, which had been so very quiet during the residence of President McKinley and his invalid wife, suddenly was filled to overflowing with the Theodore Roosevelt family. The long corridors, the stately rooms, the stairs and the elevator became the romping ground of six children (four boys and two girls) and their countless pets. They invaded every corner of the house, even exploring between the ceilings and the floors above, playing in attics which no one had entered for many years. No place was forbidden to them. Cabinet members and visiting dignitaries were often startled by encountering playful kittens and dogs and rabbits and guinea pigs, and every caller had to look carefully before sitting on a chair for fear of its being occupied by a special pet.

Alice, the eldest girl, was a young lady when the family moved in and Ted, the eldest boy, spent much time away at school. The four youngest children, Ethel, Kermit, Archie and Quentin were those who really grew up in the White House during their eight years there. Everyone loved the Roosevelts. The President was a learned man, a naturalist, a historian, and a scientist and he had a tremendous affection for and interest in his family. Mrs. Roosevelt, lovely and charming, shared his enthusiasms in all things. During their residence from 1901 to 1909 the White House was a very happy home.

All the Roosevelts loved horses and the President and his wife rode horseback almost every afternoon. Yagenka, Jocko Root, Renown, Bleistein, Wyoming, Roswell, Rusty, Grey Dawn—each had his stall in the White House stables.

The favorite of all, however, was a tiny Icelandic calico pony named Algonquin. Although Algonquin really belonged to Archie, all the children rode him. He was a spirited little animal and loved to play. One of his favorite pranks was to sneak up behind a child, lower his head and

push the child across the lawn. This was great fun for the pony, the child, and all others who watched. At other times he would attempt to throw a child from his back. Since all were good riders he did not often succeed.

Archie rode to school on Algonquin's back. Because both boy and pony were so small a man from the White House staff always rode beside them on a bicycle. The residents of Washington, hearing the sharp clippity-clip of Algonquin's hooves as they struck the road, ran to their windows to see the trio ride by. One Memorial Day, unnoticed by anyone, Archie rode his pony out of a White House gate. The street was crowded with people going to Arlington Cemetery where services were to be held for the soldiers

who had fought in America's wars. Carriages rolled across the bridge leading to Arlington, some people walked, still others rode horses, while Archie guided his tiny steed skillfully in and out among them. When he approached the cemetery entrance a sergeant on guard felt it his duty to question the boy. Upon asking him what he wanted and upon hearing Archie's reply that he wished to hear his father make a speech, the guard asked his name. The soldier then led the two aside and sent word to the White House. Someone, probably the man on the bicycle, came for them.

Once Archie had the measles. When he was recovering he longed to see his pony. He knew that his brothers and sisters were riding Algonquin and taking care of him but he felt sure that the pony missed him too. It was not enough for Archie to gaze upon the little creature from the window. His young brother Quentin also felt that perhaps Archie would get well quicker if he could hug the little animal. Waiting for a moment when no one was watching, Quentin led Algonquin into the basement of the White House, opened the elevator door and pushed the pony in. Together they went up two floors. Then Quentin opened the door and took the pony into Archie's bedroom. As Quentin expected, Archie was delighted to be able to put his arms around his faithful steed.

When the President was in the West on a hunting trip, a little black mongrel named Skip won his affection. In camp, the small fellow would sit constantly by the President's feet gazing up at him and begging to be picked up. He was a very engaging little dog and the President could not resist him. Skip always ended up curled on Mr. Roosevelt's lap while the President either wrote letters or read. When the guides called the big hunting hounds together Skip would also answer. The other dogs paid little attention to him but Skip was determined to be a hunter. He stayed close to the pack doing everything the other dogs did. He barked when they barked, sniffed when they sniffed and ran when they ran. And when the men on horseback and the baying hounds left the camp Skip would run as fast as he could to keep up with them. He scampered along beside the President's horse, looking up now and then so beseechingly that Mr. Roosevelt would finally give in and pick him up. Then Skip would ride triumphantly on the horse in front of the President. When the big hounds cornered a lynx one day Skip dashed fiercely into the fight too. Though Mr. Roosevelt wrote to Ted at home, "I do not think he is much more effective than one of your Japanese mice might be," this show of courage so captured his admiration that he took Skip back to the White House with him when his vacation was over.

Not long afterward, Skip the mongrel pup and Algonquin the calico pony became close friends. Both were so small they must have felt a kinship with each other. They had a game which they played on the White House lawn. Skip would lie quietly near the house pretending to be asleep. Algonquin, also pretending he thought Skip was asleep, would gallop around the lawn coming closer and closer to the dog. Suddenly, as though by a hidden signal, Algonquin would hesitate ever so slightly near the pup, just

enough to allow Skip to leap high in the air and land on
the pony's back. Then Algonquin would jump up and
down, shake his head and swish his tail while Skip would
hold fast barking happily all the time.

On rainy days the long halls inside the house echoed
with the shouts and laughter of the children. One of the
favorite games they played with Skip then was racing.
A child would spread his legs, throw Skip backward between them, and then run as fast as he could to the end of
the hall. Skip scrambling on the slippery floors would run
frantically to catch up and often reached the end of the
hall first. When the children were away the little dog could
not be separated from their father and he sat on the President's lap throughout many a conference.

There were other pets too. Tom Quartz was a frisky kitten who loved to tease the terrier Jack by trying to jump on him. Jack would try to keep out of the way of the kitten but Tom Quartz would seek him out. Should Tom want to have the chair in which Jack was resting, he would jump on Jack's back and the dog would dash out of the room. The only time that Tom Quartz became really subdued was the day that Quentin put him in the bathtub and turned the water on.

Sailor Boy, a Chesapeake retriever, came by his name because he was always in the boat when the children went sailing. If they forgot him he swam to the boat and jumped in while they were putting up the sail. Aside from liking water, Sailor Boy also liked gunpowder and was happiest on the occasions when the children shot off firecrackers. He was the master of all the other dogs, never allowing them to fight, nor would he himself fight unless he absolutely had to. Then his opponent was always sorry he had annoyed Sailor Boy.

Young Teddy's brilliantly colored macaw, Eli, crawled all over his master shrieking so loudly that he could be heard all through the house. Jonathan was a piebald rat who climbed up chairs and tables and people. Bill was a horned toad who lived on the south porch for many years. Once when the President stood on the platform of a train in the West, a little girl threw a baby badger to him—and the President took him home. The children named him Joshua. He was an affectionate animal and his favorite food was milk and potatoes. When playing tag with the children he sometimes nipped their bare heels. Guinea pigs were all over the place; Dewey Senior, Dewey Junior, and Bob Evans all belonged to Kermit.

All the children loved snakes, and Alice had a special favorite whom she named Emily Spinach—Emily for her aunt who was very thin, and Spinach for the snake's color which was green. Once she took Emily Spinach visiting with her and the snake got lost in the living-room curtains and later shed her skin in another room, much to the sur-

prise of her hosts. Later when Alice was to be married in the White House, among her many presents was a box of rare snakes sent by a collector.

Jonathan Edwards was a young black bear who had a bad temper and was likely to claw and bite. He was given to the Washington Zoo.

Pete, the President's bulldog, once bit a piece from the trousers of a French official who called on the President.

Squirrels, rabbits, pigs, cows, all had their turn in the family's affection. No living thing was too small or too large for the Roosevelts to love. No other President ever filled the White House with so many children, so many animals and so much happiness.

## 8: PRESIDENT HARDING AND LADDIE BOY

The editor of the Marion *Star*, weekly journal in the town of Marion, Ohio, was very angry. A puppy that belonged to a neighbor of his had been poisoned by some nameless person who was unfeeling and cruel, and the editor was doing something about it by writing his feelings on the subject into an editorial for his newspaper.

"He couldn't speak our language," he wrote, "though somehow he understood. But he could be and was eloquent with uttering eye and wagging tail and the other expressions of knowing dogs. No; perhaps he has no soul, but in these things are the essence of soul, and the spirit of lovable life.

"Whether the Creator planned it so, or enviroment and human companionship have made it so, men may learn richly through the love and fidelity of a devoted dog. Such loyalty might easily add lustre to a crown of immortality."

Editor Warren Gamaliel Harding, as he wrote these words, had no idea that he was to become the twenty-eighth President of the United States. Words he wrote from the White House were eagerly read by all peoples of the world but he often said that the editorial essay he wrote for the Marion *Star* on the death of a little dog was the best writing he ever did. It is not surprising, then, that he lavished great affection on the first gift he received after he entered the White House—a small Airedale puppy.

When Mr. Harding was elected President, and he and his wife came to live in Washington, they resolved to throw open the doors of their new home to all the people in a grand and sincere gesture of welcome. No more was the White House to be viewed with awe and from a great distance. The President and the First Lady wanted friends and they felt certain that hospitality and warmth would assure them of many.

A little precocious package, the Airedale who bore the name Caswell Laddie Boy and was the gift of Marshall Sheppey of Toledo, Ohio, "took over" within hours of his arrival and soon did much to make the Hardings new friends throughout the nation. Harding already had several dogs on the grounds, but it was the bright-eyed Airedale who made the friends and received all the invitations. Within a few short weeks Laddie Boy knew he could expect to share bits of cereal with his master each morning at breakfast. At lunch the puppy sat next to the President's chair and from time to time eagerly ate delicious morsels Mr. Harding "accidentally dropped."

As a result of his owning Laddie Boy, President Harding discovered that dog lovers from all over the United States felt as close to him as though they knew him personally. Many wrote to Laddie Boy and numbers of his admirers sent, along with their letters, beautiful and expensive gifts.

In the early spring of 1921, the Humane Education Society planned a be-kind-to-animals parade to be held in the capital and asked Mr. Harding to allow the little Airedale to lead the procession. On May 11 the streets of the capital were jammed with people, some of whom had come from nearby states to see the show. There was a long column of floats in which "Mary's Lamb" and "Black Beauty" were only two of many storybook favorites, and riding on his own float in first place was Laddie Boy, barking loudly to his master as he passed the White House.

By early summer a pure white English bulldog of celebrated lineage was made welcome in the White House. His name was "Oh Boy" and although he had been a gift to the President as early as March, he had been kept in the stables for fear he and Laddie Boy might not get on well together. By this time, however, the Airedale, having proved himself "top dog," found the company of Oh Boy a great deal of fun and so both dogs made their home with the Hardings. It was Laddie Boy, though, who brought the paper to the President every morning. The Airedale remained everyone's favorite and continued, through no pressure on his part, to make news.

In July Laddie Boy received his first birthday present. It was sent by his father, Champion Tintern Tip Top, all the way from Ohio; and though the four-tier birthday cake could have fed half the population in the capital, it appealed only to the dogs. The entire cake was composed of dog biscuits which were covered with a beautiful white icing. Oh Boy, the other dogs in the stable, and many dog neighbors came to the party and, happily ignoring the photographers, had a wonderful time.

The first sign of the President's awareness that all was not going well in his administration showed in a response Mr. Harding wrote to a note ostensibly written by a stage dog named Tiger and printed in an issue of the *National Magazine*. Tiger's letter said he was very happy to see that Laddie Boy was doing a fine job of showing to the public his loyalty and fidelity. A reply from Laddie Boy was obviously expected. Mr. Harding took it upon himself to compose a letter to which he signed his dog's name. The Airedale said that though every dog plays his part well when being his natural self, he could easily become spoiled by unfortunate surroundings and associations. Laddie Boy said, too, that many times the Chief would like to be alone with him if only to let him know of his love and to say, "Well, Laddie Boy, you and I are real friends and we will never cheat each other."

Was Mr. Harding beginning to see so soon in his term of office that the personal "friends," for whom he had obtained responsible positions, were to betray him? More and more in his loneliness and discouragement did the President feel the need for the honest love of Laddie Boy. But "man's best friend" could help little to ward off impending disaster. The very associates to whom Mr. Harding had opened his door and his heart were stealing from him his good name.

In the short time before the President's shocking and sudden death he had taken, as part of an oath of membership in an organization, a vow never to be unkind to horse or dog. This love for animals that Mr. Harding felt was neither a new thing nor an affectation. On the contrary, he found in dogs understanding and love that he never found in his relationships with his fellow men. As he had once written when he was editor of the Marion *Star*, before the burden of politics became so heavy and sad, he felt that animals were far from dumb, that they had their own way of expression.

When the President died Laddie Boy mourned in despair. Day after day he waited and watched, hoping each car that stopped at the White House would bring his master back. Mrs. Harding, her possessions packed, was preparing to leave the White House so that Calvin Coolidge, the new President, could move in and she found caring for Laddie Boy painfully sad. At length she gave the little Airedale to a man she knew would love him as much as had his late master. He was Harry Barker, a secret-service man, who wanted Laddie Boy to live with him in his home in Massachusetts.

Meanwhile a movement to make a statuette of Laddie Boy to be given to Mrs. Harding was started by Louis Newman of the Newsboys' Association. He asked that each newsboy in the nation give one penny toward the statue and in this small way pay tribute to the late President who had been for many years a newspaper man. Circulation managers of daily papers throughout the country acted

LADDIE

as custodians of the boys' contributions as they poured in.

Mr. Barker was pleased to have Laddie Boy pose for the statuette by Miss Bashka Paeff, and at the end of fifteen "sittings" it was completed. Unhappily Mrs. Harding was never to receive the statue, for she died before it could be presented to her. So the model of Laddie Boy was turned over instead to the Smithsonian Institution at Washington, D.C., where it remains as the newsboys' memorial to President Warren Harding.

## 9: THE COOLIDGE PETS

When President Harding died before his term of office had expired, Vice President Calvin Coolidge became President of the United States. The White House became the new home of Mr. and Mrs. Coolidge and family and of dozens of birds, dogs, kittens and even raccoons.

Mr. Coolidge loved animals and made it clear to his staff that all members of the animal kingdom were welcome. But it was Mrs. Coolidge who, having more hours to spare than her husband, devoted much of her time to collecting the little friends.

The birds they brought with them to the White House were two olive green canaries called Nip and Tuck. These canaries came from the Harz Mountains and they whistled and trilled their songs all day long. Gradually the Coolidges added to the bird family other feathered friends. One was a white canary named Snowflake who came from California and another a tropical bird who had been trained to sit on the shoulder of an unsuspecting guest and tweak his ear.

In almost no time at all the second floor of the executive mansion began to resemble the bird house at the zoo. Gifts sent by people who had heard of the care the President and his wife gave to their birds came pouring in from all over the world. Later additions were a yellow bird, Goldy, and a thrush who answered to the name of Old Bill. But of the many birds that lived at the White House it was the mockingbird who contributed most of the merriment. The little bird mimicked all the others and acted very much like a court jester.

It was a sad moment for the President's wife when she learned of a law in the District of Columbia which made it clear that anyone keeping a mockingbird in a cage was liable to a fine of $5 or a month in jail. Knowing how embarrassing it would be to her husband and her country to have the First Lady disobeying the law, Mrs. Coolidge parted with her favorite pet.

The next additions to the Coolidge menage were two adorable kittens. One was called Tiger and the other, a jet black furry kitten, was fittingly named Blacky. Tiger was, from the first, a wanderer, while Blacky proved himself a hunter. The first "trip" that Tiger made without informing his mistress was to the munitions building near the Lincoln Memorial. Mrs. Coolidge broadcast over radio his disappearance, giving a complete description of Tiger. Next morning a guard found him strolling unconcernedly in a corridor and, recognizing him at once, brought him back.

After this, the President decided to put collars on the cats—green for Tiger, red for Blacky—with the engraving "White House" on each collar. The collar never stopped Tiger from wandering but invariably one of the guards would find him before he roamed too far. In the spring

Blacky began to harry the birds nesting in the hedges around the east and west gardens. Several times he caught one of the baby rabbits whose mother made her home under clumps of peonies. The President and his wife took a quick vote. Blacky and Tiger were soon confined to the "guardhouse" for the remainder of the nesting season. The "guardhouse" was a well-screened patio which would now serve the dual purpose of keeping pesky mosquitoes out and pesky kittens in.

One day, after the nesting season was over and the birds and rabbits were safe, Mrs. Coolidge allowed Blacky and Tiger their freedom. Tiger seemed to have felt highly insulted by his treatment because he wandered away, never to return. Blacky, much the wiser cat, decided to make his permanent residence the White House kitchen. He had lost his taste for the wide open spaces and found the joy of having good food close by much greater.

At just about this time, when President Coolidge and his wife were beginning to feel at home in the nation's capital, they received as a present their first puppy. It was a wire-haired fox terrier named Peter Pan. Peter was extremely nervous and when he tried to bite the workmen on the White House grounds, Mrs. Coolidge was compelled to give him away. Nevertheless she and her family were not to be without a dog for long. Paul Pry, an Airedale and half-brother of Laddie Boy, the Harding dog, came to live with the new President and stayed in the kennel. Paul Pry was, as Mrs. Coolidge said, "a perfectly uncontrollable over-grown awkward puppy." She described him to friends as "the bull in the china shop." No matter how she tried to calm him and teach him to walk with the leash he continued to gallop and jump, overthrowing everything along the way, but he was so lovable it was easy to forgive him. When Mrs. Coolidge went out for even a few hours, Paul would sprawl on the carpet in her room daring anyone to touch her possessions. He was ever to be a family favorite.

The White House and its gardens were spacious and for Mrs. Coolidge and the President this was reason enough for more animals, so another puppy, sent from Wisconsin, came to the presidential mansion. His name was Rob Roy, and his ancestors had been herders of sheep. It was apparent at once that he disliked the indoors. He was frightened in the house, and he hated the White House elevator. For weeks Mrs. Coolidge coaxed him into the elevator for just a few minutes each day, talking to him gently, trying to make him understand that nothing would harm him. Soon he found the upward journey quite enjoyable. In those weeks he also found sitting in front of the fireplace a delightful experience, and after that he felt at home.

Rob Roy and Paul Pry became devoted friends. When President and Mrs. Coolidge had guests Rob would run to inform Paul and bring him into the house to share the delicacies that were being offered. One day Rob discovered that tea was being served in the Red Parlor. He ran outside for his friend but when they arrived at the parlor, they found that the food had already been set on the table. They made an attempt to eat directly from the platter but were caught by the maid, who scolded them and shoved them out. Both dogs retreated upstairs in a dignified huff.

The guards at the White House could always tell when Mr. and Mrs. Coolidge were away from the grounds, for, sprawled in front of the door lay Rob Roy sulking as though he had lost his sheep.

Rob enjoyed a game he played all by himself. He loved to bark and very often he would bark at nothing at all, as though he were letting the world know he was present. His greatest fun, however, was barking at automobiles that passed along the road. He would bark and yelp at them until he was exhausted. Then he would come back to the White House lawn and lie on the grass looking as though he had just saved the capital.

Like most dogs Rob hated his bath, and hid at the mention of the word. But when he had been washed he strutted proudly up and down the red velvet carpeted corridor.

Meanwhile Paul Pry was calming down, feeling safe in the knowledge that everyone loved him. One morning his happiness was badly shaken when he found another dog, a small Boston Bull named Beans, sitting on the lap of Mrs. Coolidge. Paul Pry pretended to ignore him but Rob Roy was very indignant. He looked at the bulldog disdainfully, dropped his tail and walked into the waiting elevator letting everyone know he had no time to waste on this interloper. Fortunately, Beans had not come to stay and in one week was on his way to a family in Northampton.

That summer Rob went with the President and Mrs. Coolidge on their vacation. Paul Pry was ill and could not make the trip. When he recovered sufficiently he was quartered with the Marines because he could no longer be trusted with the servants. Poor Paul Pry. He felt unwanted. He went to the shore and ate the dead fish that were washed up on the beach. Again he became quite sick. By the end of the summer Mr. Coolidge decided to make Paul the ship's dog but Paul would have none of it and he ran away. When he was found Mr. Coolidge gave him to the steward, who happily took him home. There, Paul Pry found what he had always wanted, small children to play with. Best of all, he was the only dog and he knew at last that he was needed.

Thanksgiving Day brought with it not only a cooked turkey but a live raccoon, a gift from an admirer. The raccoon's name was Rebecca and she was very gentle. Unlike

Rob Roy, Rebecca loved her bath and in a very little water and with a big piece of soap the raccoon would play for hours. She was given the run of the White House and delighted the many visitors who came to see the President.

At about this time a beautiful white collie—"breaker of hearts" as Mrs. Coolidge said of her, came to live at the White House to keep Rob Roy company after his friend Paul Pry had left. Mrs. Coolidge named the collie Prudence Prim but called her Prudy. Everyone loved Prudy. She was gentle and cuddly and anxious to please. Prudence Prim and Rob Roy became fast friends and made a handsome couple. Prudy was perfectly happy in the drawing room and when tea was served she moved from guest to guest munching quietly on some tidbit as she welcomed each one. In the living room, when the family was present, she found herself a favorite window recess and remained there calmly watching everything that went on. Rob meanwhile sat in another window spot watching Prudence.

In a moment away from her chores Mrs. Coolidge made a bonnet of straw and trimmed it with maidenhair fern and green ribbons for Prudy. She tied the bonnet under Prudy's chin and the collie wore it to one of the garden parties the First Lady gave for the soldiers. Of course Prudence made a tremendous hit and she knew it. She loved to wear the bonnet and felt that it was meant for her. Mrs. Coolidge always referred to the bonnet as "Prudy's hat." But Prudence Prim was never a very healthy dog and in spite of all the care she received, she died young.

To help Mrs. Coolidge forget Prudy a friend gave her a

three-month-old chow. His name was Tiny Tim and he was
round and fat and red-haired. Tiny Tim slept on a blanket
next to Mrs. Coolidge's bed. In about four weeks Tiny
Tim outgrew his name, so Mr. Coolidge changed it to Ter-
rible Tim, which fitted his temperament more accurately.

At this time another white collie pup came to the White
House. Her name was Calamity Jane and she made the
trip from the West to the capital in an airplane. When she
arrived her thick fur had collected machine grease in the
plane and she cried and cried. She made her home in the
kennel with another new addition, a white and tan collie
whose name was Ruby Rough.

There were several other dogs in the White House kennel
during Mr. Coolidge's term as President of the United
States, but Prudy, Rob and Paul always remained the
very special pets.

During their last years in the capital Mrs. Coolidge made
gifts to the zoo of a bear which someone had sent from
Mexico and a whole family of chickens which had the
honor of staying temporarily in the President's bathtub for
want of a better place.

When Mr. and Mrs. Coolidge said good-by to the White
House after Mr. Coolidge had served six years as President,
they gave Calamity Jane, no more the crybaby puppy, to
a guard. Another dog, King Cole, was given to a school-
teacher in Kentucky. It is probable that during Calvin
Coolidge's years in the capital more dogs and cats had a
happy home in the White House than at any other time in
the history of our country.

## 10: FALA

Perhaps the most widely discussed pet that ever lived in the White House was a little Scotty, black as the ace of spades and just as important. His real name was Murray the Outlaw of Fala Hill, reduced, for the sake of convenience, to Fala. He was a very little puppy when Margaret "Daisy" Suckley decided he would make a wonderful gift for her cousin Franklin Delano Roosevelt. The President was delighted with him. Master and puppy were sure at once that they were going to be great friends and the first time the President patted Fala's head and whispered "Good doggie, good doggie," they knew the friendship would blossom into love.

Fala's stay in the White House is, to date, one of the longest in the history of our country because his master, who became known throughout the world simply as F.D.R., was elected by the people to serve as President of the United States four consecutive times.

The years of his presidency were trying years for both the President and the people of the nation. They were years of hardship and years of promise. They were years of peace and years of war. And through them all there were many moments of love and tenderness that the great man shared with his faithful Fala. No matter how many papers there were to be signed or how many guests to greet, the little Scotty was always close by. He would watch the President carefully and when company got ready to leave he would bound out of the corner and be first at the door. At this point, F.D.R., a victim of polio since he was thirty-nine, would lean over his wheel chair and ask, "Fala, do you want to go out?" knowing full well what Fala's answer would be. Of course Fala, as he always did, would run out the door, down the steps, and jump into the front seat of a waiting car. There he would sit, stubby tail wagging expectantly, waiting for his master to join him in the hoped-for drive. Fala's bushy black head was soon recognizable throughout the countryside. Indeed, it was troublesome at times keeping the whereabouts of the President a secret because Fala's presence always gave it away.

Fala had several beautiful places he was able to call home. The one he seemed to enjoy most was Hyde Park, the lovely old New York State house which lies on a green rise overlooking the Hudson. Hyde Park, charming, warm, always open to friends and neighbors, constantly buzzing with activity and cheer, belonged to the Roosevelt family for many years. This was home for F.D.R., the house in which he was born and which held all the familiar childhood memories.

It was here that the President went for most of his vacations and holidays. The President's room, like nearly all the rooms, remained almost exactly as it had been when he was a boy. It was Fala's room too, for he slept on his own navy blanket beside his master. At Hyde Park the family felt closer and more relaxed. Even though the President conducted his business as usual in a small ground-floor room, which became world famous as the "Summer White House," Fala and his master had more time to play. Each evening at teatime the President, much to everyone's delight, fed Fala tidbits meant for the guests. It was a private joke between the master and his beloved Scotty and, as a result, the tea hour became President Roosevelt's favorite time of day.

During the cold winter months the President and his family, which included his secretaries, "Missy LeHand and Grace Tully," and Fala would go to still another home in Warm Springs, Georgia. In Warm Springs F.D.R. bathed in the sulphur-bearing water and exercised his paralyzed legs. Polio victims from all over the world came to Warm Springs, not only to soothe sick limbs, but to gather courage from the man who had courage to spare. And, as in all the places where Fala lived, he made many new and lasting friends.

Back at the White House in Washington, Fala's biggest problem was having to share the President with so many strangers. There were times when the little Scotty must have thought he was forgotten. Of course this could never be. The President was constantly busy with guests from all parts of the world, who came to hear reassuring words of hope and who brought with them words of praise for the President from their home countries. Many times Missy

LeHand would gently but firmly pat little Fala out of the room so that the President would not be distracted by his frisky movements. So, to Fala, the big White House meant more and more work for F.D.R. and less and less play for them both.

One day when the President's gracious wife Eleanor returned from a diplomatic mission she received an urgent message summoning her to the President's side. She was worried, for this had not happened before. She was sure the President must be very ill. She rushed into the conference room where her husband gave her a quick nod and handed her a slip of paper. F.D.R., on seeing her look of bewilderment, hurried to explain. Fala had been ill while she was away and so he had called a veterinarian, who had prescribed medicine and a special diet for the Scotty. Would Eleanor please see that the diet listed on the paper she now held in her hand was provided by the cook so that Falla would get better soon? Mrs. Roosevelt, always patient and understanding, smiled. She was quite sure that this was the first time F.D.R. had ever been aware that any "member" of his family was in need of a special diet.

Fala was the President's constant companion on his trips around the country. They rode in a special train which accommodated members of the Cabinet, private secretaries, visiting dignitaries and reporters from all the important newspapers. When the train made its stops at various stations, some newspaper reporter traveling with the party was invariably asked to walk Fala. Politics were at a standstill during these moments while Fala and his friend ran up and down unfamiliar streets.

In 1944, during the exciting presidential campaign in which F.D.R. ran for his fourth term against Thomas E. Dewey, politics and puppy mixed. Poor Fala became the target of accusations and abuse. He was blamed for taking up needed space on planes, trains and boats. Indeed, he was blamed for an unnecessarily high budget. If Fala tossed his black head in indifference, his master did not. In one of his now famous fireside speeches President Roosevelt let the country know that certain people were calling Fala names and Fala didn't like it. In his inimitable way F.D.R. put his finger on all the attacks that were being circulated by his enemies. So, once more, F.D.R. and Fala had their private little joke.

The proud Scotty and his famous master, however, were soon to be parted. In the middle of April, 1945, news of the President's sudden and unexpected death shook the nation. The millions of friends he had made during his long term in office were stunned with grief, his loved ones heartbroken. That afternoon Fala had sat alert but quiet in a corner of the bedroom not daring to move. When the doctor had pronounced the President dead, he leaped from the corner, crashed through a screen door, barking wildly till he reached the top of a nearby hill. There sad Fala stood vigil.

So far as the dog was concerned, F.D.R. was not the President of the United States, nor was he the Commander in Chief. He was a master—kind, understanding, loving. To Fala, the little black Scotty who lived in the White House, F.D.R. was his closest friend.

## 11: MORE HAPPY COMPANIONS

President James Monroe and his family were the first to live in the new residence built on the site of the burned-down "palace" whence the Madisons had fled on the night that the British armies captured Washington. The White House, as it soon came to be called, was elaborately decorated in the "French manner" and its contents were so precious and so delicate that it was hardly a proper place for a romping little girl. Maria Hester Monroe was twelve years old when her father was elected to the presidency and she was far from quiet and inactive.

When the prominent Judge Tucker of Virginia had visited the Monroes in Washington eight years before they moved into the White House he had noted two things about the three-year-old Maria Hester. The first was that she was wearing pantalettes beneath her skirts, introducing a new style which the judge recommended in a letter to his daughter for her own little girl, and the second, her dog. Wrote the judge of Maria Hester: "The little monkey did not fail to evince the advantage of her dress. She had a small Spaniel dog with whom she was continually engaged in a trial of skill—and the general opinion seemed to be that

she turned and twisted more than the Spaniel." Whether she had the lively little dog with her when she went to live at the new White House does not seem to be known.

During the administration of John Quincy Adams, Gen-

eral Lafayette visited the White House in July and August, 1825. On his long tour of the United States he had been presented with a live alligator. He kept the animal in the East Room where it frequently caused unsuspecting visitors moments of panic. He was much more unpleasant than the mulberry-leaf-fed worms raised in the White House to provide Mrs. Adams with cocoons from which she unwound strands of shining silk, but not as much of a problem as two ferocious tigers presented by an Indian potentate to Martin Van Buren when he was President.

Before Andrew Jackson became President, like many another general, he had become fond of horses. He had raced his famous stallion Truxton against almost as well known Greyhound in 1805. In 1811 his Doublehead had defeated Colonel Newton Cannon's Swift Expectation at Jackson's own Clover Bottom Track. When he lived in the White House there were three racing fillies in the White House stables—Emily, Lady Nashville and Bolivia. When they were entered in competitions, their ownership was usually attributed to the President's son-in-law, A. J. Donelson, in order to avoid the criticism that it would be undignified for the President to be engaged in horse-racing. The Negro jockeys did their best with Mr. Jackson's horses but none of them succeeded in winning an important race.

Thomas Jefferson had seen to it that a cow barn sheltered his cows, which he kept for producing milk for the daily

needs of his family and guests, and the presence of cows grazing on the White House lawn was accepted and approved by the public (who liked the homely farm touch) throughout many administrations.

Andrew Johnson, who became President after the assassination of Abraham Lincoln, was a man of simple tastes and he and his wife tried to live in the White House much as they had in rural Tennessee. Their daughter Martha, who had married Senator Patterson of her home state, purchased two Jersey cows, famous for their thick creamy milk. Like all good Tennessee farm girls, Martha got up before sunrise to do her chores. Clad in a calico dress and a big gaily printed apron, she would hurry from the White House to the barn to superintend the skimming of the wrinkling yellow cream from the top of wide shallow milk pans and perform her other duties in the dairy before breakfast. She was very proud of the modern equipment of the dairy and visitors there always found crocks, pans, and churns in apple-pie order.

Frances Folsom, the young and beautiful Buffalo girl who married President Grover Cleveland in the White House on June 2, 1886, was a Wells College graduate who had acquired a very special interest in birds. Canaries twittered and sang throughout the White House during her husband's two administrations. Like Martha Washington and Thomas Jefferson she was fond of mockingbirds and one of these lovely singers was a favored pet though not always as much of a delight to the serious, hard-working President.

One night when Mr. Cleveland was attempting to solve a particularly perplexing problem in the White House library, the mocker chose to sing long and loud, interrupting the work in progress time and again. Knowing his young wife's love of the bird Mr. Cleveland stood the annoyance as long as he could, then summoned Thomas Pendel, the White House doorkeeper, who happened to be still awake, though the time was between one and two in the morning.

"Pendel," said the President, "I wish you would take that mockingbird down. It annoys me." Mr. Pendel took the bird in its cage to a spot some distance away and afterward reported in his published reminiscences the bird was so offended that it stopped singing. The silence that followed made the President even more uncomfortable than the singing. Knowing how much his beloved bride treasured her pet he became more and more nervous. Finally he said, "Pendel, where did you put him?" "On Mr. Loeffler's desk," said Pendel. "You don't think he will catch cold there, do you?" said Mr. Cleveland and Mr. Pendel replied, "Mr. President, I don't think he will but, however, I will move him."

This time the servant carried the bird to an inner corridor of the White House and placed it behind a screen where no draft could reach it. When Mr. Cleveland had finished his work Pendel reported, "Mr. President, I have put him behind here where he will not catch cold."

"Oh, that is all right, Mr. Pendel," said weary Mr. Cleveland and he happily climbed the stairs to bed.

Of other Presidents, none have had pets exciting enough to inspire stories of their worthy but rather colorless activities. President Rutherford B. Hayes had a strong interest in farm animals, and his herd of pedigreed Jersey cows, his team of spirited carriage horses, his dogs and his chickens were all greatly admired.

President Benjamin Harrison brought his daughter, Mary Harrison McKee, to the White House and provided her son with a kennelful of dogs and a well-groomed billy goat.

President William H. Taft's cow, Pauline Wayne, achieved an uncertain immortality through a portrait photograph for which the State-War-Navy Building served as a background.

Woodrow Wilson's sheep, which kept the White House lawn well clipped, were regarded as the most patriotic on record when they contributed during World War I ninety-eight pounds of wool which, sold at auction for the benefit of the Red Cross, brought that worthy organization a hundred thousand dollars.

Herbert Hoover's police dog, King Tut, is said to have been muzzled because of his overzealous guarding of the White House from people he regarded as unfit to enter the grounds, and to have died of mortification as a result.

Harry Truman was presented with a small dog named

Feller who, according to daughter Margaret's account, never amounted to much.

And finally President Dwight D. Eisenhower in his second administration acquired a big and beautiful ginger-

colored Weimaraner puppy named Heidi. She gave but one press conference at which she was presented with a life membership in the Washington Tailwaggers Club. She seemed so overwhelmed (or possibly so crestfallen) by this procedure that, forgetting the dignity of her station and ignoring Mrs. Eisenhower's command to sit, she jumped on the president of the Tailwaggers, almost causing a loss of equilibrum. Mrs. Eisenhower tactfully explained, "She is so nervous," and her secretary finally persuaded Heidi to sit for the photographers.